Unhinged:
The Impact of
Trump Derangement
Syndrome on
American Society

Proudly Presented By:
- JWH Jr.

Table of Contents

Introduction:

The term "Trump Derangement Syndrome" (TDS) emerged as a provocative way to describe the intense and often irrational reaction many individuals displayed in response to the presidency of Donald J. Trump. Originally coined in political discussions to suggest that opponents of Trump suffered from a form of cognitive dissonance, TDS became shorthand for a phenomenon far more complex than mere partisan sentiment. It encapsulated a time when the fabric of American society appeared stretched to its limits, revealing deep fissures in ideology, discourse, and communal cohesion.

By exploring this condition, we venture into the heart of America's current socio-political climate, touching on themes of identity, belonging, and the powerful role emotions play in shaping political landscapes. TDS represents a divergence of beliefs, an exaggerated response often fueled by an unrelenting barrage of news, opinions, and social media posts that create echo chambers. Individuals on both sides of the political spectrum have manifested symptoms of this syndrome, demonstrating that the impacts of TDS reach beyond mere political disagreements—they penetrate the very core of how we understand ourselves in relation to one another.

In an increasingly digital age, the cacophony of voices has made it challenging to discern truth from hyperbole, leading to a society where feelings often take precedence over facts. Emotional responses, especially those elicited by Trump's presidency, have often spiraled into name-calling, vitriol, and division, stifling any meaningful conversation about policy or governance. This tension begs the question: what has happened to our national discourse? Are we capable of rational discussion, or have we succumbed to a pervasive state of emotional turmoil?

The various sections of this book will serve as a map for navigating the tumultuous waters of contemporary American society defined by TDS. We will begin by tracing the origins and the evolution of the term itself, delving into how it became a cultural touchstone. From there, we will investigate how the political landscape has shifted during and after Trump's time in office, highlighting the fissures that have formed in an already divided nation.

We will also examine the pivotal role of media—both traditional and social—in amplifying the effects of TDS. The dual forces of clickbait journalism and the echo chamber effects of social media have created environments where hyper-partisanship thrives, stifling constructive exchange. Psychologically, the symptoms of TDS connect to broader trends, including anxiety, anger, and a sense of dislocation, influencing not only individual psychological well-being but also societal mental health.

Furthermore, we will explore how TDS has written itself into contemporary cultural narratives—shaping literature, art, and public expression in myriad ways. It invites a critical examination of cultural resistance and acceptance alongside an evaluation of communal dialogue.

In the latter sections, we will present case studies that shine a light on personal stories of TDS, illustrating the complexities of real human experiences. In closing, we'll strive to identify pathways toward healing, recognizing that while the divisions are significant, understanding and dialogue remain vital tools for restoring a healthy public discourse.

Ultimately, "Unhinged: The Impact of Trump Derangement Syndrome on American Society" aims not just to reflect on a troubling chapter of American political life, but to foster understanding and reconciliation in a fractured landscape. In doing so, it seeks to pave the way for a new era of discussion—one that values reason, compassion, and, ultimately, healing.

Chapter 1: The Genesis of Trump Derangement Syndrome

The political landscape in the United States has experienced seismic shifts over the last two decades, with Donald Trump's ascent to the presidency marking one of the most significant transformations in recent history. To understand Trump Derangement Syndrome (TDS), we must first grasp the complex dynamics at play during this transitional period, characterized not only by Trump's unique brand of politics but also the reaction it evoked across the political spectrum.

Historically, the term "derangement syndrome" had been applied to various political figures to describe a perceived irrational response to their actions. The phrase found a renewed popularity during the era of Trump's presidency, capturing the emotions of a significant segment of the population who believed that Trump represented existential threats to democracy, societal norms, and global stability. The hyperbolic nature of this response led some defenders of Trump to label the reaction as "deranged," prompting conversations that rarely, if ever, led to mutual understanding.

In political discourse, the methodology often consists of framing differences through a binary lens, especially in a hyper-polarized landscape. For many, the term TDS symbolizes the challenge of engaging with a political opponent or critic of Trump without devolving into tribalism—a fundamental aspect of modern American politics. This chapter aims to explore the emergence of TDS through a careful examination of its origins, implications, and consequences.

The genesis of TDS can be traced back to the initial stages of Trump's candidacy in 2015 when he mobilized a politically disenchanted base with his unorthodox rhetoric and promises to "drain the swamp" of Washington politics. His unconventional communication style, marked by tweets and offhand remarks, alienated traditional political discourse while simultaneously invigorating supporters who appreciated his candid, sometimes provocative, approach. However, this very style activated a defensive posture among critics who perceived him as an existential threat.

As Trump transitioned from candidate to president post-2016, reactions intensified. Public discourse became charged, creating a landscape where measured discussion gave way to outrage. Political commentary shifted from analysis to condemnation, and attitudes toward Trump often became imbued with personal animus rather than policy disagreement. The notion of TDS effectively captured this phenomenon —characterizing an emotional reaction perceived by supporters as an irrational fixation that overshadowed political realities.

To frame this discussion, it is essential to recognize that TDS doesn't only reside among those vehemently against Trump. Within his base, a sense of allegiance emerged that produced a counter-derangement sentiment—an unwavering loyalty that was equally as impassioned, producing various manifestations of denial or minimization regarding Trump's failings. In many cases, facts were bent or obscured through a lens of loyalty and affection that defied conventional notions of political accountability.

This emotional rawness has significant implications for understanding the contours of political discourse. As heightened emotional stakes lead to polarized environments, rational discussion becomes an increasingly rare commodity. Public debate starts to mirror personal grievance, where the questions of "What does this mean for me?" or "Whom should I blame?" emerge, transforming political engagement into a battleground of grievances.

The prevalence of TDS also intersects with the rise of social media platforms, which have transformed how political discourse unfolds. Social media creates an amplifying mechanism whereby sensationalism often dethrones rationality. The consequences are profound: emotional reactions fire up algorithms, facilitating the spread of polarizing content that exacerbates tensions. In a media environment designed for engagement rather than enlightenment, individuals gravitate towards content that reinforces their biases, further entrenching the divides that TDS symbolizes.

One must also consider the psychological aspects of TDS. While some critics dismiss TDS as mere hyperbole, those wrestling with its effects often describe feelings of anxiety, frustration, and despair. Psychological research indicates that extreme political emotions can lead to physical health issues, interpersonal discord, and a pervasive sense of hopelessness. Understanding these emotional dimensions is crucial not just for comprehending TDS, but also for devising potential pathways for recovery and understanding.

In many ways, TDS embodies an urgency for introspection and reconsolidation of political dialogue. It calls for individuals to examine their emotional responses to political figures critically. Are we functioning as rational beings motivated by policy and principles, or have we allowed ourselves to become ensnared in a web of emotional reactions that inhibit constructive engagement?

Thus, the journey begins: in dissecting political derangement, we shall seek to illuminate the complexities at play, delve into the nuanced dimensions that characterize this fervent emotional response, and pave the way for a deeper understanding of how TDS has redefined American politics, interaction, and civil discourse.

Chapter 2: The Political Landscape: A Divided Nation

As the 2020 presidential election approached, the United States appeared to be a nation on the brink—politically fractured and ideologically polarized. The term "Trump Derangement Syndrome" encapsulated a burgeoning cultural rift, where the mere mention of Trump elicited strong reactions and provoked fervent debate on all fronts. To understand TDS, one must explore how this division came to fruition against a backdrop of uncertainty, shifting values, and a complex electoral landscape.

The seeds of polarization were visible long before Trump's entry into the political arena. The aftermath of the 2008 financial crisis led many to question the efficacy of established political systems and practices. Distrust in government institutions began to swell, ushering in movements—from the Tea Party to Occupy Wall Street—marked by a growing dissatisfaction with traditional forms of governance. Within this setting of discontent, Trump's populist messaging gained traction, resonating with disenfranchised voters desperate for change.

Moreover, the 2016 election was a defining moment, largely driven by identity politics that saw both the Republican and Democratic parties in reactive states. Trump's candidacy brought longstanding racial, economic, and cultural tensions to the forefront, creating a situation where the stakes felt incredibly high. For many, supporting Trump symbolized not only a departure from established political norms but also a rejection of the prevailing cultural conversations about race, gender, and identity. Those who viewed Trump as a threat to social progress found themselves battling an opponent whose rhetoric galvanized supporters and shifted the narrative around political dialogue.

On the opposing side of this political spectrum, resistance to Trump accelerated the phenomenon of TDS. The emotionality surrounding his policies and remarks catalyzed a cycle of outrage that frequently led to disillusionment and hopelessness. For many critics, the fabric of democracy felt jeopardized by unprecedented actions such as the dismissal of the rule of law, widespread misinformation, and incendiary rhetoric. This sentiment was amplified by many advocacy groups, celebrities, and media figures who engaged in condemnatory rhetoric that often overlooked constructive, bipartisan dialogue.

While TDS is used to describe those perceived as overreacting to Trump's actions, it also points to a broader tendency to demonize political opponents—in this case, those who either supported or defended Trump. Biased portrayals of "Trumpers" created caricatures that dismissed their perspectives entirely. This reductionist view often resulted in further entrenchment on both sides, as individuals grew comfortable within their ideologies, shielded from opposing viewpoints by social and political bubbles.

To understand the impact of TDS on the political landscape, one must delve into the emergence of platforms and movements that catered exclusively to segmented audiences. Social media transformed how information and opinions circulated, creating echo chambers where validation replaced critique. This enabled individuals to consume content that reinforced their pre-existing beliefs, further entrenching divisions.

The technological landscape contributed to this rapid disintegration of discourse. Platforms like Facebook and Twitter became conduits for divisive rhetoric, often celebrating virality over accuracy. The algorithms that drive engagement disproportionately favored sensational, emotionally charged content. As shared outrage gained traction, the quality of discussion diminished, echoing the sentiments of TDS where emotional resonance overshadowed rational debate. The national stage became one of psychological warfare, where memes replaced measured political discourse, sows further discord between divided sects.

Moreover, this emotional engagement often intersects with wellness and mental health discussions. Surveys indicate growing anxiety tied to the political climate, with many individuals expressing feelings of helplessness and dread in facing the nation's trajectory. A notion that strikes fear into the hearts of many is the idea that the very essence of the American identity is under siege. As these feelings percolate through society, they foster an atmosphere where rational discussion about policies, governance, and solutions feels elusive.

Throughout the 2020 election period, distinctions blurred even further, as the line between partisan loyalty and personal identity blurred. Individuals began to associate core identity traits with their political affiliations, with aversion becoming the default response to those who disagreed. This shift raised significant concerns about civil discourse in an era where belonging to a political tribe feels integral to one's sense of self.

In this polarized environment, the very notion of compromise became radical. Afghan historian, Dr. Khalid Nabavi, succinctly stated that "in the modern political arena, compromise threatens purity." Such sentiments saw interactions evolve as both sides trained their focus outward, unmooring themselves from the pursuit of common ground.

As the chapters unfold and the illusions of TDS become clearer, we shall explore how we got here. It is a call to examine not just the manifestations of derangement, but the underlying societal fractures that fuel those reactions. Understanding the political landscape of contemporary America, with its accompanying tensions and emotional stakes, is pivotal to reshaping our collective future.

Chapter 3: Media Frenzy: Amplifying the Chaos

In an age defined by rapid technological advancements, the role of media—both traditional and social—has undergone a profound transformation that amplifies societal tensions and accelerates the phenomenon known as Trump Derangement Syndrome (TDS). The digital era has ushered in an unprecedented democratization of information dissemination, making news accessible at lightning speed while simultaneously cultivating a breeding ground for misinformation, outrage, and polarization.

Historically, news media served as a crucial intermediary, shaping public discourse and informing citizens about governance, policies, and cultural developments. However, the advent of the internet and, subsequently, social media has fundamentally altered that landscape, resulting in a paradigm shift characterized by the immediacy of reporting and the sensationalization of events. The pre-2016 media landscape featured reputable journalistic standards that aimed to provide balanced perspectives, but increasing competition for viewership and clicks soon grew to eclipse such ethical considerations.

The intensity of Trump's presidency magnified these changes, with every tweet, rally, and presidential statement becoming fodder for media coverage that often lacked nuance. The rush to report on Trump's actions led to a cycle in which sensationalism triumphed over context; a single inflammatory statement could dominate headlines, and analyses often got relegated to the background. This hyper-focus on individual actions obscured deeper conversations regarding policies and governance, narrowing the channels through which political discourse typically flowed.

A major aspect of this media frenzy is the role of partisan news outlets that emerged in response to the divisive political landscape. Networks such as Fox News and MSNBC quickly polarized viewers, demonstrating the power of framing in shaping perception. For many audiences, how news was presented became intrinsically tied to identity. Viewers selected outlets that aligned with their beliefs, promoting a filter-bubble effect that reinforced preexisting biases. Rather than functioning as tools for understanding diverse perspectives, these platforms became instruments for validation, aggrandizing tribalism in political affiliations.

Critically, this formation of ideological media "clubs" further contributed to the development of TDS. As viewers surrounded themselves with content that reaffirmed their beliefs, those opposing Trump were often painted as irrational, mitigating anything within the realm of testimony that indicated support or appreciation for his administration. Thus, the outrage was deepened; the ability to engage constructively with differing opinions became more challenging. Cross-party dialogues shifted to confrontational exchanges rooted in contempt rather than reason.

The role of social media deserves particular attention in this context. Platforms like Facebook, Twitter, and Instagram transformed the landscape of political conversation, enabling individuals to disseminate opinions freely while simultaneously molding public discourse. The viral nature of posts encouraged users to amplify audio-visual content that elicited strong emotional reactions, often prioritizing sensationalism over substance. This framework not only heightened the visibility of conflicting perspectives but also entrenched divisions as users gravitated toward outrage-filled narratives that vilified the opposing side.

Moreover, the 2016 election saw a surge in the influence of influential factions, conspiracy theories, and the dissemination of misinformation, laying the groundwork for a media ecosystem fuelled by suspicion. The prevalence of "fake news" became a pivotal narrative, permeating public consciousness and creating an environment where distrust flourished. This further complicated narratives surrounding TDS, as phrases like "fake news" were weaponized to delegitimize media sources, blur lines of truth, and foster skepticism.

As the 2020 election unfolded, the stakes escalated, catapulting Trump's rhetoric into the digital limelight, and the phenomenon of outrage became the hallmark of media engagement. Events—such as the Capitol riot on January 6, 2021—confirmed fears of a media landscape that prioritized sensationalism above all else. Disinformation about voting processes and election integrity reverberated across platforms, leading to a public that increasingly distrusted conventional media.

While TDS has often been portrayed as an emotional condition, examining its origins necessitates a deeper understanding of how our media consumption shapes public perception and emotional response. Researchers have identified undeniable correlations between emotional news consumption and mental health; intense exposure to negative news can exacerbate feelings of anxiety and helplessness. In turn, such anxiety heights the likelihood of extreme reactions—propagating a cycle that fuels TDS.

The disconnection between rational critique and emotional engagement raises critical questions about the future of political discourse. As public figures decry sensationalist coverage, how do we reconstruct narratives that foster understanding? Examining how media frenzy influences TDS emphasizes the need for a more deliberate, conscientious approach to consumption and engagement, acknowledging the pervasive influence of tech and emotion-driven networks.

Furthermore, the shifting landscape of media consumption also demands personal responsibility. The emotional weight carried by TDS offers significant insights into the way political dialogues can spiral into chaos, illustrating how deeply intertwined emotional health and media are within the broader political framework. Here lies an opportunity for individuals to actively engage in balancing their media diet, seeking out factual, balanced opinions while refraining from engaging solely in outrage-driven narratives.

In its entirety, the media frenzy surrounding Trump Derangement Syndrome has illuminated the fractures within our political fabric. As we navigate the complexities of this modern media-driven age, it becomes increasingly necessary to reevaluate our relationship with information. Finding a balance between access and accountability, discourse and decency, and narrative and neutrality may prove instrumental in steering our collective consciousness away from chaos and towards a more coherent, productive space for dialogue.

Chapter 4: Psychological Perspectives: Understanding the Reaction

As the phenomenon of Trump Derangement Syndrome (TDS) continues to evolve, one aspect warrants close examination: the psychological dimensions underlying the reactions individuals experience in response to Donald Trump's presidency. TDS is not merely a buzzword; it evokes powerful emotions that can profoundly impact mental health, relationships, and political engagement. By delving into these dimensions, we can gain insights into why some individuals react with overwhelming intensity while others appear immune to such emotional upheaval.

At the core of TDS lies a complex interplay of emotions that manifest as anger, anxiety, and hopelessness. These feelings stem from both personal and collective experiences of disillusionment with the political process, raising challenges surrounding identity, belonging, and social trust. Understanding these emotional responses requires exploring how deeply ingrained political beliefs and individual psychological frameworks shape reactions to political figures like Trump.

One framework of psychological inquiry that illuminates TDS is Cognitive Dissonance Theory. Proposed by Leon Festinger in 1957, this theory posits that individuals strive for harmony between their beliefs and behavior. When confronted with information that conflicts with established beliefs (in this case, support or opposition to Trump), cognitive dissonance occurs. This discomfort prompts individuals to either change their beliefs, justify their existing beliefs despite evidence to the contrary, or reframe the information to align with their viewpoints.

For those entrenched in their dislike of Trump, exposure to his rhetoric, policies, or supporters can elicit significant cognitive dissonance. The dissonance manifests as frustration, as individuals struggle to reconcile their emotional reactions with the realities of a Trump presidency. The psychological energy expended in navigating this conflict can lead to heightened awareness of not only political events but also a profound sense of alienation from those who hold differing beliefs.

Conversely, supporters of Trump may also encounter cognitive dissonance when reconciling their admiration for him with the criticisms levied by detractors. The phenomenon of "confirmation bias"—where individuals favor information that aligns with their beliefs—heightens the likelihood of dismissing opposing viewpoints entirely, often labeling critics as victims of TDS. This creates a cycle where individuals on both sides of the political spectrum become ensnared in spirals of emotional distress fueled by a lack of meaningful discourse.

Another crucial psychological component of TDS is the concept of "ingroup" versus "outgroup" dynamics. In psychology, ingroups refer to groups with which individuals identify, while outgroups refer to those perceived as outsiders. Research has consistently demonstrated that ingroup loyalty significantly influences emotions, beliefs, and behaviors. In the context of TDS, criticisms against Trump evoke strong ingroup identification among his supporters, who often view attacks on him as attacks on themselves—a protective mechanism that fosters an emotional defensiveness across political lines.

Additionally, social identity theory postulates that individuals derive a sense of self-worth from their group affiliations. For many, political allegiance becomes entrenched in their social identity, leading to heightened sensitivity when their political beliefs are challenged. Confrontations over Trump often incite fierce reactions, as seemingly benign exchanges can evoke feelings of vulnerability or betrayal—particularly when challenging views are voiced by friends or family. This context exacerbates the emotional stakes attached to political discussion, making debate feel less like an exchange of ideas and more like a personal affront.

The implications of mental health in the context of TDS cannot be overlooked. Research indicates that excessive exposure to contentious political discourse can result in psychological distress, manifesting as anxiety, depression, and relational struggles. Many individuals grapple with a sense of helplessness when confronted with a political landscape that appears increasingly volatile and dysfunctional. In many ways, TDS has fostered a culture of despair where individuals continually refresh social media feeds, seeking validation yet finding only further polarization.

Furthermore, the cycle of emotional distress often leads to social withdrawal, isolation, and difficulty participating in civic engagement. Those experiencing TDS may feel disconnected from friends or family who hold opposing views, leading to a fragmentation of relationships and a retreat into spaces of like-minded supporters. Such disconnection encourages further isolation from valuable perspectives, further entrenching individuals within their emotional states and beliefs.

Despite the deeply rooted nature of TDS, psychological insights can also illuminate pathways for potential healing and understanding. By fostering dialogues rooted in empathy and active listening, individuals can begin to navigate the emotions surrounding political discourse in more constructive ways. Recognizing the emotional dimensions inherent within TDS can become a valuable step toward healing not just individuals but the broader societal divide.

Innovative approaches to emotional intelligence and resilience can provide valuable tools for engaging with differing opinions. Discussions surrounding psychological safety, boundary-setting, and critical thinking can cultivate environments where dialogue flourishes. By situating political conversations within frameworks of respect and emotional understanding, individuals can gradually navigate the turbulent waters of TDS while fostering connections and newfound perspectives.

The relationship between TDS and psychological well-being underscores the urgent need for self-reflection and introspection. As individuals grapple with their emotional responses to Trump or any political figure, understanding the psychological impacts of these reactions can inform approaches for personal growth and bridge-buiding across divides.

As we continue to explore the implications of TDS on American society, it is essential to maintain a commitment to understanding ourselves and each other. Acknowledging the emotional stakes tied to political beliefs, tempered by psychological insight, can pave the way for richer discussions and solutions. In turn, this lakes the jumble of distrust, fear, and animosity, laying the groundwork for more humane and constructive conversations, bridging the gaping divide that TDS represents.

Chapter 5: Cultural Ramifications: Art, Literature, and Expression

In examining the multifaceted landscape of Trump Derangement Syndrome (TDS), we must not overlook the pivotal cultural ramifications it has wrought upon art, literature, and broader expressions of societal sentiment. As a phenomenon reverberating through public consciousness, TDS has ignited a firestorm of creativity, activism, and cultural resistance. Artists, writers, and creators from various disciplines have responded in profound ways, crafting works that reflect the complexities of contemporary politics while confronting the emotional turmoil that TDS evokes.

The genesis of TDS opened up new avenues for cultural production—serving as the backdrop for a wave of creative expression that critiques, satirizes, and reflects on the political climate. In many ways, the conditions surrounding TDS triggered a renaissance of political art, where artists harnessed their mediums to confront the tensions characterized by Trump's presidency and to navigate the psychological landscapes it engendered.

One particularly striking characteristic of this cultural output is the resurgence of satire and humor—artistic tools historically employed to challenge authority and confront societal injustices. Political satire flourished in the digital age, with comedians, cartoonists, and writers unleashing scathing critiques on Trump and his policies. Late-night talk shows emerged as prominent platforms for exploring the absurdity of the political climate, amplifying the voice of satire as a means of coping with uncertainty and chaos.

Iconic figures like Stephen Colbert, John Oliver, and Trevor Noah became assimilators of outrage, merging entertainment with analysis as they navigated the nuances of TDS. The fusion of humor and critique served to create a shared communal experience where audiences could process their frustrations through laughter—an acknowledgment of the absurdities of their political landscape that often obscured the underlying tensions. Through satire, artists allowed for a release of pent-up emotions and offered audiences a mirror through which to examine not only the political but also their own reactions.

Moreover, literature has become a critical vehicle for exploring the psychological and emotional dimensions of TDS. Writers leveraged the narrative richness of fiction and nonfiction to articulate the disarray and fracture that permeate contemporary society. Books that tackle the psychological undercurrents of a politically charged America, such as novels, essays, and memoirs, have emerged as cultural artifacts representative of the zeitgeist.

Contemporary authors capitalized on their platforms to share deeply personal accounts and reflections, mapping the journey of individuals wrestling with TDS. Works like "What Happened" by Hillary Clinton and "The Room Where It Happened" by John Bolton serve as touchstones in understanding the emotional reverberations that the political landscape produced. The value of literature lies in its capacity to humanize the political conversation—to confront the emotional fallout associated with TDS, allowing readers to grapple with their own experiences in a relatable manner.

Public art has also burgeoned in the wake of TDS, with protests serving as canvases for political expression. Street art, murals, and installations emerged as provocative commentaries on Trump's presidency, asserting space as a medium for dissent and social justice. A notable example is the prolific work of artists like Shepard Fairey—whose iconic "Hope" poster of Barack Obama paved the way for a larger movement—capably adapted to challenge the current administration through striking and subversive imagery.

These artistic endeavors are often fraught with intensity. Many artists have called upon their audiences to confront uncomfortable truths, using the provocative nature of their work to invite discussions about race, gender, and inequality—themes rapidly foregrounded by Trump's ascent. The complexities of political representation create fertile ground for conversation and action, with cultural products instigating a dialogue around what it means to engage responsibly in a contentious political environment.

The cultural ramifications of TDS extend into the realm of activism, where art becomes a clarion call for social change. For many creators, the emotional experiences associated with TDS demand action beyond expression. Numerous grassroots movements have employed culture as a tool for organizing, leveraging art and literature to galvanize community action. The Women's March in January 2017 heralded a potent coming-together of artistic expression, as creative placards coupled with powerful performances sparked waves of mobilization against perceived injustice.

Furthermore, the impact of TDS on cultural production encourages introspection regarding identity and representation. The disruptions in political landscapes have fostered renewed conversations about marginalization, privilege, and authenticity within cultural narratives. A diverse array of voices emerged to share varied experiences related to TDS, highlighting the importance of intersectionality in art and literature.

As creators reflect on their position within society, the very act of cultural production becomes a political act. The relationships between audience, creator, and contextual awareness create powerful exchanges rooted in emotion, engagement, and visibility. Such explorations illuminate both personal and collective experiences that shape responses to societal upheaval.

Ultimately, the cultural responses to TDS mirror the complexities of the human experience when tethered to the turbulence of politics. Artists and creators across disciplines engage in a profound dialogue about the emotional stakes surrounding Trump—a reckoning that extends beyond mere discourse and into the transformative possibilities of art, literature, and activism.

As we move through the complexities of TDS and its resonance in contemporary society, the cultural dimensions remind us of the profound capacity of art and expression. While the emotional response to TDS may be complex, we witness a tapestry of creativity that invites reflection, challenges perspectives, and inspires action. This dynamic interplay between art and politics underscores the journey toward capturing cultural narratives, contributing to the ongoing conversation about healing and understanding in emotionally charged times.

Chapter 6: Social Media and the Echo Chamber Effect

In the modern political era, social media has reshaped the way individuals communicate and engage with political discourse, effectively embedding itself within the contours of Trump Derangement Syndrome (TDS). Platforms like Twitter, Facebook, and Instagram have amplified the effects of TDS through the creation of echo chambers—digital environments where users are insulated from opposing viewpoints, fostering heightened polarization and emotional confrontation.

The emergence of social media as a dominant communication tool has transformed political engagement from localized discussions to global conversations, allowing individuals to connect across vast distances and share information instantaneously. However, this democratization of information has not come without a price: the algorithms deployed by these social media platforms often prioritize content that aligns with users' beliefs, exacerbating divisions and heightening tribalism.

At the heart of the echo chamber effect is the phenomenon of confirmation bias—the tendency to seek out information that aligns with preexisting beliefs while avoiding conflicting perspectives. Research consistently shows that social media users gravitate towards groups or pages that resonate with their views and values, creating insulated spaces where challenging ideas are dismissed rather than engaged. In this context, TDS manifests as an emotional response to that perceived threat, often resulting in fervent, exaggerated outrage directed at political figures, policies, or those with divergent opinions.

Moreover, the design of social media platforms favors engagement over accuracy. Posts that trigger strong emotions—whether positive or negative—generate more engagement than reasoned, balanced discourse. This deeply affects users' perceptions of political events, framing discussions through a lens of outrage rather than authenticity. As emotionally charged content becomes the norm, individuals find themselves immersed in an environment where the parameters of political discourse narrow, leading to an increased likelihood of viewing opponents through a lens of derangement.

The implications of the echo chamber effect extend far beyond mere political disagreement, permeating personal relationships and community dynamics. As individuals become enmeshed in their respective online tribes, the likelihood of encountering alternative viewpoints diminishes significantly. Friendships and familial bonds can strain as political discussions devolve into emotionally fraught confrontations. Individuals often feel compelled to sever ties with those seen as "other," choosing instead to engage primarily within echo chambers that reinforce their identities and beliefs.

The proliferation of misinformation within these echo chambers further complicates the landscape of TDS. In an environment where outrageous claims can go viral at lightning speed, false narratives can take root and persist, shaping public perceptions and chilling constructive conversation. The media landscape surrounding Trump is fraught with disinformation, including absurd conspiracy theories that cater to specific ideological narratives. The intertwining of misinformation with confirmed beliefs contributes to heightened emotions, resulting in reactions that can be categorized as symptomatic of TDS.

Research into the psychological impacts of social media shows a correlation between heightened screen time, outrage, and declining mental health. For many users, excessive exposure to politically charged content fosters feelings of despair, anger, and helplessness—further revealing the emotional stakes bound to TDS. Engagement with social media becomes a source of anxiety, as users feel compelled to continuously check in for updates and outrages, perpetuating a cycle of emotional turmoil that mirrors the political divide.

However, the role of social media cannot be seen solely as a catalyst for division; it also acts as a platform for mobilization, activism, and cross-ideological engagement. Movements such as #MeToo and Black Lives Matter have successfully utilized social media to galvanize support, share stories, and promote social justice causes. While social media contributes to polarized opinions, it can also foster community building and facilitate constructive dialogue among diverse individuals, creating spaces for empathy and understanding.

In grappling with the echoes of TDS within social media, we arrive at crucial questions regarding our responsibility as engaged citizens. How can individuals navigate digital landscapes without sacrificing their emotional well-being, relationships, and, ultimately, society as a whole? Reclaiming social media requires deliberate efforts to foster understanding, counter misinformation, and open channels for dialogue.

Critical media literacy emerges as a vital tool in addressing the rampant misinformation prevalent in social media environments. Educating individuals about identifying credible sources, recognizing biases, and engaging with diverse perspectives can empower users to traverse echo chambers with nuance. Initiatives that promote conscious media consumption encourage individuals to recognize their own biases, mitigate isolation, and cultivate productive conversations across digital platforms.

Moreover, social media platforms must bear some responsibility for the content that circulates within their networks. The role of regulation and the ethical ramifications of algorithmic promotion cannot be ignored, as tech companies grapple with the implications of perpetuating divisive narratives. Transparency, accountability, and ethical engagement between platforms and users are pivotal in creating healthier digital landscapes.

Ultimately, to navigate the emotional turbulence surrounding TDS, individuals must reinvigorate their commitment to critical thinking, civil discourse, and respectful engagement—both online and offline. Recognizing the profound power of social media as both a tool of division and a platform for connection sets the stage for a more empathetic public dialogue that prioritizes understanding rather than derangement. Cultivating emotional intelligence and maintaining a conscious media diet can empower individuals to challenge the narratives that perpetuate tribalism while fostering bridges across political divides.

As we explore the ramifications of the echo chamber effect, we are confronted with the dynamic interplay between our online behaviors, emotional reactions, and political views. The challenges posed by TDS call upon all of us to engage thoughtfully in the pursuit of informed dialogue and mutual understanding. In doing so, we can rewrite the narrative of TDS, transforming it from a symbol of division to an opportunity for connection, learning, and growth.

Chapter 7: Case Studies: TDS in Action

To comprehensively understand the multifaceted dynamics of Trump Derangement Syndrome (TDS), we must examine the real-world instances where these phenomena converge, illustrating both the emotional stakes involved and their implications for society. This chapter presents multiple case studies that underscore the manifestations of TDS, revealing how personal experiences, significant events, and communal reactions intertwine to create a complex tapestry of outrage and discontent.

Case Study 1: The Kavanaugh Hearings

The confirmation hearings of Supreme Court Justice Brett Kavanaugh in 2018 marked a critical moment in the TDS narrative. The hearings were not merely a judicial appointment; they represented broader societal tensions surrounding gender, power, and personal accountability. As allegations of sexual assault surfaced against Kavanaugh, responses varied dramatically along partisan lines. For many supporters of Kavanaugh, the accusations were perceived as an attack on the legitimacy of his candidacy—leading to calls of political derangement among those who opposed him.

Conversely, those who believed the allegations saw Kavanaugh's ascendance as an affront to the principles of justice and a reaffirmation of patriarchal structures. The emotional stakes intensified as protests erupted on the Capitol steps and social media became inundated with conversations that oscillated between support for victims' rights and the defense of the accused. The hearings encapsulated not only TDS but also illustrated the profound divide within American society over issues such as sexual harassment, gender equality, and the judicial system's accountability.

As accusations emerged, fervent responses proliferated on both ends of the political spectrum. Social media became a battleground where emotions flared, evoking panic, rage, and disappointment. Users amplified personal accounts, echoing outrage at the perceived injustice of Kavanaugh's confirmation, while defenders framed responses as indicative of a deranged "liberal mob" intent on obstructing justice. The hearings left scars on relationships and communities from which they would not quickly recover, underscoring how TDS manifests in heightened emotional responses spiraling into entrenched divisions.

Case Study 2: Charlottesville and the Rise of Extremism

The tragic events that unfolded in Charlottesville, Virginia, in August 2017 may serve as one of the most egregious examples of TDS in action. The rally organized by white supremacist groups unveiled not only the persistence of systemic racism in American society but also elicited polarized responses that further exemplified TDS. The incident claimed the life of Heather Heyer and injured multiple others, inciting national outrage and triggering deep societal divides.

Upon condemnation of the rally by politicians and citizens alike, the stark contrast in responses from Trump supporters and critics illuminated the underlying psychological complexities tied to TDS. Critics of Trump pointed to his subsequent comments regarding the "very fine people on both sides" as evidence of a failure to rebuke white distorted the truth while stifling discourse on free speech. Many viewed criticisms of Trump as a manifestation of TDS—angry, irrational reactiosupremacy and a perpetuation of hate speech. For many, this moment crystallized their detestation of his rhetoric and policies, giving rise to heated emotions felt across the country.

Conversely, supporters rallied around Trump's comments, interpreting them through a lens of victimhood, as if to suggest that liberal medians to a president seeking to navigate a turbulent political landscape. This divergence in interpretation exacerbated the already palpable tensions in American society, as public discussions devolved into emotional outbursts, suspicions, and a lack of empathy for the opposing perspective.

In the aftermath of Charlottesville, communities witnessed a ripple effect of moral outrage, protests, and counters to movements advocating for equality. The event ultimately became a social touchstone, shaping conversations about race relations, freedom of speech, and the fragility of democracy in contemporary America—illustrating the extensive emotional investment associated with TDS and the risks it poses to public discourse.

Case Study 3: The 2020 Presidential Election

The 2020 presidential election cycle epitomized a manifestation of TDS on a grand scale, as reactions to Trump intensified amid widespread social unrest and a pandemic that reshaped daily life. As ballots were cast against the backdrop of protests for racial justice, individuals on both sides of the political spectrum engaged fervently in the dialogue surrounding the election, often with heightened emotions that reflected the stakes involved.

Part of the remarkable tension stemmed from the unprecedented polarization that characterized the election season. Supporters of Joe Biden rallied behind notions of restoring integrity, morality, and hope in government, with many viewing Trump's presidency as an assault on democracy itself. Claims of oppression, fear, and mistrust dominated social media platforms as narratives surrounding the election spiraled into emotional landscapes fraught with uncertainty.

In contrast, Trump supporters framed the election through the lens of patriotism, resisting what they perceived as an attack on their way of life. The mistrust of voting systems prompted responses anywhere from protests to allegations of election fraud, fostering outrage rooted in a perceived assault on democratic values. Digital communities reinforced these sentiments, with numerous patterns of misinformation sowing discord and fear.

The socio-political environment bore witness to violent confrontations between protestors and counter-protestors, illustrating the extent of division fueled by emotional responses tethered to TDS. Many individuals felt compelled to advocate for their beliefs passionately, as the election became an emotional battleground enmeshed in disputes over identity, ideology, and representation. From the battleground states to the online forums, the struggle for dominance became visceral and, at times, devastatingly personal—yielding a heightened awareness of how deeply TDS infused the political conversation.

As these case studies illuminate, TDS manifests variedly in real-world contexts, underscoring both its rampant emotional stakes and communal divides. The interplay of personal experiences, media narratives, and socio-political landscapes generates emotions that color how individuals engage with politics, often drawing them into polarized landscapes where outrage replaces reasoned discourse.

This chapter has sought to dissect TDS through tangible examples that highlight the emotional and social ramifications inherent within the phenomenon. As we continue to navigate a complex political world, recognizing these case studies empowers us to seek constructive responses—acknowledging that our emotional connections to political figures and events are not monolithic but deeply intertwined with our shared humanity.

Chapter 8: Moving Forward: Healing a Divided Society

As we emerge from an era marked by the tumultuous impact of Trump Derangement Syndrome (TDS), it becomes evident that addressing the emotional fallout and societal fractures that it has instigated will be crucial in forging pathways toward collective healing and understanding. The polarization that has proliferated in recent years challenges our ability to engage with differing perspectives, compelling us to reconsider not only our political affiliations but also the manner in which we communicate with one another.

The journey toward healing begins with acknowledgment. It is essential to recognize the emotional weight carried by many in the wake of TDS, elucidating that frustrations and anger are not solely the domain of one political camp. Across the political spectrum, individuals have navigated feelings of helplessness, anxiety, and disillusionment. These sentiments must be validated and brought into broader conversations surrounding not only TDS but also the nature of effective political discourse and governance.

One pivotal step toward bridging divided communities entails fostering respectful dialogue—an approach characterized by active listening, empathy, and a commitment to understanding the complexities of differing perspectives. Encouraging individuals to engage in civil discourse does not mean abandoning one's beliefs; instead, it invites deeper consideration of how those beliefs shape interactions with others. Before entering conversations as adversaries, individuals must endeavor to relate on a human level.

Dialogue frameworks that prioritize understanding can help mitigate the emotional turbulence characteristic of TDS. Initiatives aimed at facilitating difficult conversations, such as community dialogues or workshops focusing on conflict resolution, allow individuals to grapple with their emotions and perceptions in spaces designed for empathy. Additionally, incorporating mindfulness practices into discourse can change the narrative; encouraging individuals to pause, reflect, and approach discussions from a place of understanding can build healthier means of engagement.

Furthermore, as our political landscape continues to diversify, it is vital to embrace inclusivity within these conversations. Recognizing the intersections of race, gender, and socio-economic status enriches dialogues and fosters unity in addressing shared goals. The collective effort of voices from marginalized communities can engender new understandings of political issues, allowing us to recognize TDS not as an isolated phenomenon but as part of a broader socio-political context that demands multifaceted approaches.

Education plays a crucial role in the effort to heal a divided society. Broadening the scope of political education enables individuals to develop the skills necessary to critically engage with diverse perspectives. Incorporating curriculums that emphasize media literacy, critical thinking, and historical context in schools can empower students to become informed and engaged citizens better equipped to navigate the complexities of political environments.

Equally important is the role of media organizations, which bear a responsibility to regain public trust by committing themselves to ethical journalism and accuracy. Restoring integrity in reporting entails cultivating journalistic standards that prioritize factual information, compassionate storytelling, and a commitment to pluralism in narrative. The media landscape cannot merely vilify the other side; it should balance criticism with opportunities for understanding, thereby contextualizing narratives within a larger dialogue about human experience.

Additionally, social media platforms have a significant role to play in mitigating the divisive effects of echo chambers. Rather than emphasizing engagement solely for profit, social media companies must invest in technologies that promote diverse viewpoints and provide users with the tools to distinguish misinformation from credible information. Initiatives that reward critical engagement can redirect users away from sensationalism and toward meaningful inquiry; hence, they can help combat the emotional turmoil produced by TDS.

On an individual level, one of the most powerful tools we possess is the capacity for empathy. Simple acts of compassion—such as reaching out to those with differing opinions or offering support during emotionally fraught discussions—can dismantle barriers that perpetuate division. Individuals can strive to resist assumptions that solely categorize opponents as deranged and instead approach conversations with an open heart and mind.

Lastly, community-building efforts serve as quintessential pathways toward healing and cohesion. Engaging in local initiatives, volunteering, or participating in community forums fosters connections that transcend political divides. The very act of coming together, whether through shared interests, goals, or challenges, builds a foundation of trust and understanding that can mitigate the emotional strains of TDS.

Ultimately, the journey toward healing a divided society in the aftermath of TDS is challenging yet necessary. As we face the emotional stakes tied to our political beliefs, we must challenge ourselves to engage with empathy, understanding, and vulnerability. The realities of TDS serve as a sobering reminder of the consequences of disconnection but also as an opportunity for reconnection—the potential to reframe our national conversation toward one marked by compassion, inclusivity, and mutual respect.

As we close the pages of "Unhinged: The Impact of Trump Derangement Syndrome on American Society," it is my hope that this exploration incites reflection, dialogue, and a renewed commitment to healing the fractures that have defined recent political history. It is only by working together—beyond the chaos of derangement—that we can endeavor to forge a brighter, more unified future.